How To Use Response Cost

Susan F. Thibadeau

How To Manage Behavior Series

R. Vance Hall
and
Marilyn L. Hall
Series Editors

pro·ed
An International Publisher
8700 Shoal Creek Boulevard
Austin, Texas 78757-6897
800/897-3202 Fax 800/397-7633
Order online at http://www.proedinc.com

An International Publisher

8700 Shoal Creek Boulevard
Austin, Texas 78757-6897
800/897-3202 Fax 800/397-7633
Order online at http://www.proedinc.com

Library of Congress Cataloging-in-Publication Data

Thibadeau, Susan F.
    How to use response cost / Susan F. Thibadeau.
       p.   cm.—(How to manage behavior series)
    Includes bibliographical references.
    ISBN 0-89079-762-5 (paperback : alk. paper)
    1. Behavior modification. 2. Punishment (Psychology) I. Title.
  II. Series.
LB1060.2.T55   1998
371.39'3—dc21   97-43041
                                                  CIP

This book is designed in Palatino and Frutiger.

Production Director: Alan Grimes
Production Coordinator: Karen Swain
Managing Editor: Chris Olson
Art Director: Thomas Barkley
Designer: Lee Anne Landry
Staff Copyeditor: Suzi Hunn
Reprints Buyer: Alicia Woods
Preproduction Coordinator: Chris Anne Worsham
Project Editor: Debra Berman
Production Assistant: Dolly Fisk Jackson
Publishing Assistant: John Means Cooper

Printed in the United States of America

2   3   4   5   6   7   8   9   10   02   01   00   99

Contents

Preface to Series

The first edition of the *How To Manage Behavior Series* was launched some 15 years ago in response to a perceived need for teaching aids that could be used by therapists and trainers. The widespread demand for the series has demonstrated the need by therapists and trainers for nontechnical materials for training and treatment aids for parents, teachers, and students. Publication of this revised series includes many updated titles of the original series. In addition, several new titles have been added, largely in response to therapists and trainers who have used the series. A few titles of the original series that proved to be in less demand have been replaced. We hope the new titles will increase the usefulness of the series.

The editors are indebted to Steven Mathews, Vice President of PRO-ED, who was instrumental in the production of the revised series, as was Robert K. Hoyt, Jr. of H & H Enterprises in producing the original version.

These books are designed to teach practitioners, including parents, specific behavioral procedures to use in managing the behaviors of children, students, and other persons whose behavior may be creating disruption or interference at home, at school, or on the job. The books are nontechnical, step-by-step instructional manuals that define the procedure, provide numerous examples, and allow the reader to make oral or written responses.

The exercises in these books are designed to be used under the direction of someone (usually a professional) with a background in the behavioral principles and procedures on which the techniques are based.

The booklets in the series are similar in format but are flexible enough to be adapted to a number of different teaching situations and training environments.

R. Vance Hall, PhD, is Senior Scientist Emeritus of The Bureau of Child Research and Professor Emeritus of Human Development and Family Life and Special Education at the University of Kansas. He was a pioneer in carrying out behavioral research in classrooms and in homes. Marilyn L. Hall, EdD, taught and carried out research in regular and special public school classrooms. While at the University of Kansas, she developed programs for training parents to use systematic behavior change procedures and was a successful behavior therapist specializing in child management and marriage relationships.

As always, we invite your comments, suggestions, and questions. We are always happy to hear of your successes in changing your own behaviors and the behaviors of other persons to make your lives more pleasant, productive, and purposeful.

R. Vance Hall &
Marilyn L. Hall,
Series Editors

How To Manage Behavior Series

How To Maintain Behavior

How To Motivate Others Through Feedback

How To Negotiate a Behavioral Contract

How To Select Reinforcers

How To Teach Social Skills

How To Teach Through Modeling and Imitation

How To Use Group Contingencies

How To Use Planned Ignoring

How To Use Prompts To Initiate Behavior

How To Use Response Cost

How To Use Systematic Attention and Approval

How To Use Time-Out

Introduction

This book is intended as a guide for parents, teachers, and other professionals as they work to shape and improve the behavior of their children, students, or others. While positive consequences effectively strengthen and maintain desirable behaviors, there are times when additional consequences may be appropriate to reduce unwanted behavior. One such consequence is response cost.

The reader will learn the sequence of steps to follow in order to use response cost in an effective and responsible manner. The examples provided are culled from a body of research in applied behavior analysis and the author's own experiences. As the reader progresses through the book, he or she will probably recognize examples of response cost from his or her own life. Exercises are also placed throughout the manual to guide the reader in understanding and applying response cost in the home, work, or community environment.

The procedures and exercises are designed to be used under the supervision of a professional with a strong behavioral background, someone who can provide guidance to the reader should he or she encounter problems or need suggestions.

Why Should You Consider Response Cost?

Every person, whether it be in the role of professional, family member, or friend, is confronted with behavior he or she would like to change. Behaviors that jeopardize one's health and safety, that detract from a pleasant social or work environment, that interfere with one's learning or attending to task, or that negatively impact on the greater good, are all issues of concern. Although one can work toward changing behaviors using a positive approach, it is sometimes necessary to apply negative consequences to behavior in order to bring about more rapid change.

The elementary school-age child who frequently yells out in class and pushes other children on the playground displays behaviors that require immediate intervention. The adolescent who skips school at an increasing rate and is beginning to participate in illegal activities demands attention as quickly as possible. The adult who repeatedly violates driving regulations must experience a significant consequence in order to change this behavior. In each of these cases, one may need to impose some fine or loss of privileges

Susan Thibadeau is the Director of the May Center for Child Development in Chatham, Mass., a program of the May Institute, providing special education services to children and adolescents with autism and behavior disorders. She is also an Adjunct Associate Professor in the special education department at Fitchburg State College. She has served as a consultant to special education programs and as an expert witness for the U.S. Department of Justice.

to have the desired reductive effect on these disruptive and potentially harmful behaviors.

Although more significant or aversive consequences may be applied, response cost offers an alternative approach that can effect change without seriously disrupting or isolating the individual.

What Is Response Cost?

In Preschool

Emily and Alice were playing with the collection of toy animals in one area of the preschool classroom. The teachers were pleased to see the level of cooperation, as Alice could often be too aggressive when seeking out her preferred toys. Just as one of the teachers decided to approach the girls to provide Alice with some positive feedback, Alice grabbed the lion out of Emily's hand. Now, instead of offering praise to Alice, the teacher quietly took the toy from her and returned it to Emily. Alice protested, but the next time Emily had an animal she wanted, she offered to exchange her elephant for Emily's giraffe.

In High School

Jake was very excited the day of the game. The skies were clear, there were scouts in attendance, and he was looking forward to the homecoming celebrations that would continue later that afternoon. The team was behind by 4 points with 1½ minutes remaining in the last quarter of the game. Jake was sure they would score a touchdown as they were within 5 yards of the goal line and with such a sufficient amount of time left, there was little reason to be concerned. Then he made a mistake. As a tackle from the opposing team was about to sack the quarterback, Jake reached out and grabbed the first thing his hand contacted. Regrettably, it was his opponent's face mask and Jake knew full well that he had just caused the team to lose 15 yards. There was little time left and now the team had 20 yards to gain to win the game. Although Jake played more carefully, making no further mistakes, in the end the game was lost.

In College

Hannah had signed up for 18 credit hours this semester. Although she realized this was a heavier course load than she was used to, she was determined not only to complete the requirements for her bachelor's degree by May but also to maintain her 3.5 cumulative average. All of her work had been turned in except the take-home final for the economics course, which had proven to be her most difficult. The professor had warned the class that 5 points would be deducted from a student's grade for each day that the final was late. Hannah struggled to meet the deadline, but arrived too late to the professor's office. As it turned out, her loss of these 5 points resulted in her cumulative average slipping to a 3.4. She vowed that when she began graduate school she would manage her time better.

In a Work Setting

Tom was driving home from work after a long but rewarding day. He had finally convinced the other members of the board to agree to his proposal of giving employees 3 extra days of vacation time for every 2 days they performed volunteer service in the local community. Tom had always viewed the community as supportive of his business and he was determined to show his thanks by giving something valuable to the neighborhood. As he drove along the highway, anxious to get home to share the news with his family, he didn't notice that he was traveling 10 miles above the speed limit. He was shaken out of his thoughts when, in his rearview mirror, he noticed the blue lights approaching. Although the officer was polite as Tom explained that driving too fast was out of character for him, he still handed over a ticket with an accompanying fine of $50. His perfect day was not going to end on a perfect note.

In each of these examples, a form of response cost was in place to help change one's behavior. Response cost involves the removal of some portion of reinforcement contingent upon or immediately following a specific, unwanted behavior. Typically this contingent loss of reinforcement involves penalties, fines, or loss of items or points. The person is not removed from the activity, but rather must forfeit part of the reinforcement otherwise available.

_____

For each of the examples provided above, please identify the reinforcer that was removed.

Alice: _____

_____

Jake: _____

_____

Hannah: _____

_____

(continues)

Tom: _____

_____

If you indicated Alice's loss of the lion, Jake's loss of yards gained, Hannah's loss of points, and Tom's loss of $50, you were right. These are all examples of response cost that occur in daily lives.

In the following sections, I describe response cost in greater detail. As stated previously, response cost involves the loss of some quantity of positive reinforcement contingent upon an identified behavior. The individual may experience a loss of privileges, a loss of money, or a loss of points or tokens.

Contingent Loss of Privileges

Response cost can be very simple to implement when the targeted behavior leads to the loss of a specific privilege, activity, or object. For example, elementary school teachers have often made recess contingent upon specified appropriate behavior, such as completion of assigned work. If the work is not completed, the student experiences a loss of recess. Others have used loss of free time as a form of response cost. In a study conducted by Rapport, Murphy, and Bailey (1982), response cost procedures were found to be even more effective than medication in improving the classroom performance of two boys identified as hyperactive. During response cost, the boys were told that they could earn 20 minutes of free time for attending to their assignments during two 20-minute independent work periods. The teacher would subtract 1 minute of free time whenever the child was observed to be off-task. For both students their time on task and their correct performance on the task improved most dramatically under response cost conditions.

An interesting application of response cost was demonstrated by Piazza and Fisher (1991), who were working with children with developmental disabilities who experienced sleep problems. Improvements in sleeping were observed after bedtimes were gradually faded and a response cost was imposed. In this instance, the children were removed from bed for 1 hour if they did not fall asleep within 15 minutes of lying down in bed. Thus, the response cost was loss of time lying in bed.

Contingent Loss of Money

In other situations, it is neither possible nor desirable to remove the privilege contingent upon the targeted response. The librarian does not wish to eliminate one's access to the library because of overdue books, yet there is the goal to impress upon all borrowers an awareness and courtesy toward others with regard to the timely return of material. The insurance company would go out of business were it to withdraw the coverage of everyone who was a few days late with payment, yet for the company to continue operating, the timely receipt of bills is essential. In each of these cases, a fine is imposed for late return or payment, maintaining customers while helping to improve their behavior.

Problems shared by many families are the difficulties associated with shopping trips. Children may wander to look for items, pick up items that are not to be purchased, or complain about being bored. One interesting treatment package (Clark et al., 1977) provided families with guidelines to address many of these behaviors. Specifically, parents were advised to inform their children at the start of the trip that they had $.50 of their allowance to spend when the shopping was completed. Further explanation was provided that each rule violation resulted in the loss of a nickel. This strategy proved to be very effective, resulting in dramatic reductions in the problem behaviors.

This form of response cost has also been demonstrated to be effective with adults in a work setting. Three agencies of one state participated in a study designed to increase the use of seatbelts among state employees when using agency vehicles (Rogers, Rogers, Bailey, Runkle, & Moore, 1988). All vehicles were equipped with stickers that informed employees of the risk of a 25% reduction in benefits provided by worker's compensation if they were involved in an accident and were not wearing a seatbelt. Two of the groups were also informed of this policy in a memo, which they were expected to sign. The result was a dramatic improvement in seatbelt use while using state vehicles.

Contingent Loss of Points or Tokens

Tokens are exchangeable items that help bridge the gap between the demonstration or occurrence of an appropriate response and some tangible reinforcer. These are extremely useful in bringing about behavior change as the individual can be provided with positive feedback immediately without significant disruption to the ongoing activity. For example, a preschool student can receive a sticker during circle time for following an instruction given to the group while continuing to participate. This sticker can later be traded for some special privilege, such as holding the door open for classmates going outside. The high school student can earn 5 points for raising his hand to respond to a question and later trade points earned for time out of study hall. While these are examples of awarding tokens for positive behavior, many token programs also incorporate response cost strategies to enhance their effectiveness. (See Ayllon & McKittrick, 1982, and Kazdin, 1985, 1989 for detailed reviews of token economies.)

At a program for adjudicated youth, an elaborate token economy was developed to change the behavior patterns of teenagers living in a group home setting (Phillips, 1968; Phillips, Phillips, Fixsen, & Wolf, 1971). Staff members were taught to award points for appropriate behavior, including prompt arrival to meals, maintenance of a clean room, engagement in study programs, and so on. In at least one case, Phillips and his colleagues demonstrated the added benefit of a response cost component when employing a token economy. As a means of developing appropriate school behaviors and conversation skills, the group home staff began awarding points to students who correctly answered questions about stories presented during the evening news. It was not until these students also lost points for not responding correctly to a designated percentage of questions that a significant increase in correct responding was noted. Others have demonstrated a similar enhancement of the effectiveness of a token program when response cost is added to it.

Response cost in the form of token loss has also been applied within the business community. In an effort to improve safe working practices in mines, Fox, Hopkins, and Anger (1987) developed a token economy in which trading stamps could be earned each month if the employee had not suffered any injuries or caused damage to equipment. Contingencies were in place to award both the individual and the group. Conversely, stamps could be lost if injuries or damages did occur. The outcome was a significant reduction in personal injury and property damage as a result of unsafe practices.

Define **response cost:** _____

_____

_____

_____

_____

Did you note that response cost involves the loss of some amount of positive reinforcement following a specific, unwanted behavior? If so, you have provided an accurate definition. If you added that this could involve the loss of an item, activity, privilege, amount of money, or number of points, you have provided an even more detailed definition.

Considering your own experiences, provide three examples of response cost.

1. _____

_____

(continues)

2. _____

   _____

3. _____

   _____

Basic Steps in Using Response Cost

▶ **Step 1: Specify or define the behavior you want to change.**

As with any treatment strategy, it is important that you first identify what it is you would like to change. People you care about, individuals with whom you work, people you rely upon for services, all may at one time or another exhibit behavior that you consider to be inappropriate. Before you can try to change the behavior, however, it is important that you specify what it is you want to change. For example, although you may think your child is impolite to relatives, politeness is a very broad concept that often holds very different meaning to different people. If you think about it, you may realize that all you really want is for your child to say hello while looking at a guest in your home, before running off to play. This is a much clearer description than "polite" behavior.

Mrs. Wang was a special education teacher who worked with high school students who were at risk of dropping out or failing school. Many of these students exhibited behaviors that were often described as disrespectful and unacceptable in the secondary education setting. These behaviors included swearing, fighting, tardiness, and unexcused absence from school. Mrs. Wang decided to begin to make changes by starting with a behavior that occurred in school and that she believed was the easiest to define: tardiness. She quickly realized, however, that her definition of "late to class" was very different from her students' definition. Therefore, she established the following rule: As the bell signaling the start of class began to ring, she would start her stopwatch. Any student who was inside the classroom within 60 seconds was on time. Anyone outside the classroom or arriving to class after 60 seconds was considered late. This proved to be a clear definition to all those involved.

Read the following example and then write a definition of Kevin's problem behavior based on the information given.

Kevin was a third-grade student who had been diagnosed with autism. He would interact with his peers to a limited degree and could make his point with spoken language. However, when his goals were frustrated, either because he could not adequately explain what it was he wanted or because he did not want to wait his turn, he would sometimes hit, pinch, or pull the hair of another student. His teacher, Mr. Matthews, was concerned about this behavior, not only because it caused harm to his other students but also because it made social skill development that much more difficult for Kevin. Mr. Matthews decided that he would develop a point system to help change Kevin's aggressive behavior; however, he first needed to define the behavior he wanted to change.

Write a behavior definition: _____

_____

_____

_____

_____

_____

If your definition reads something like, "Aggression is defined as anytime Kevin hits, pinches, or pulls the hair of another person while at school (both inside and outside on the playground)," you've done well. Remember, though, that this would not include any aggression observed on the bus.

One problem encountered when defining unwanted behavior is the use of terms that imply negative attributes of the individual. For example, people may be described as angry, unmotivated, or antisocial. These terms do not describe observable behavior, nor do they specify the behavior that needs to change.

When Stella met her new teacher, Ms. Cummings, she told her, "I don't do math." Ms. Cummings was surprised at this introduction, but Stella's teacher from last year had warned her that she was "arrogant" and "opposi-tional." Ms. Cummings had decided to ignore these descriptors and to take a wait-and-see approach. The first day had progressed nicely until math class. When Ms. Cummings handed Stella her math book, Stella threw it to the floor, loudly proclaimed that she was not going to do any work, and then put her head down on her desk.

How do you think Ms. Cummings defined Stella's problem behavior?

_____

_____

_____

_____

If you listed the observable behaviors that Stella exhibited, including throwing her book to the floor, stating that she was not going to work, and putting her head on her desk, you're right.

Now, think of two individuals with whom you have daily or weekly contact and who exhibit a behavior you would like to change. Provide a specific description or definition of the behavior. To help, think about *who* is exhibiting *what* behavior, then think about *where* and *when* you observe this response.

Behavior 1: _____

_____

_____

_____

Behavior 2: _____

_____

_____

_____

(*continues*)

Are your definitions written so that anyone, after reading your descriptions, would be able to point out the behaviors when they occurred? If so, you're on the right track. If not, go back and try again, remembering to describe the behavior in clearly observable terms while answering the questions who, what, where, and when.

▶ **Step 2: Assess the behavior.**

To clearly understand the current rate of a behavior, it is important to measure it before beginning any treatment. This is necessary and important for at least two reasons. First, you may be pleasantly surprised to find that the behavior is not occurring as frequently as you thought. The problem may be much less serious and/or may in fact not be a problem at all. Second, collecting an initial measure of the behavior provides you with a barometer against which you can compare the behavior once you begin treatment. This allows you to objectively determine whether what you are doing is having the desired effect. This initial measure of the behavior is referred to as *baseline*.

Several measurement systems are available. I will review a few options, but you are directed to *Behavior Analysis for Lasting Change*, (Sulzer-Azaroff & Mayer, 1991) for a more thorough review of measurement possibilities.

Permanent Product

This type of measurement system can be used when the behavior results in a concrete product that lasts over time. Examples of behaviors that are amenable to permanent product recording include the number of action verbs written in a story, the number of toys left on the floor of the room, or the number of lights left on at work.

Frequency of Event

You might choose to count the number of times the behavior occurs within a set period of time. When using this measurement system, you identify a specific period of time (e.g., ½ hour, 2 hours) during which you will tally the number of occurrences of the targeted response. This can be a fairly easy procedure to use with those behaviors that have clear beginning and ending points (e.g., hitting, swearing, taking items without permission, asking for assistance).

Rate

You might find that you are more interested in measuring the frequency of the behavior during a specific activity (e.g., meals, shopping trips). The actual time involved varies. Here you would tally the number of occurrences as you did above; however, you would then divide this number by the number of minutes the activity consumed.

Duration

Another alternative is to time the length of the behavior. If time is a critical element (e.g., you want to reduce the amount of time your teenage daughter spends in the bathroom each morning), this is a viable measurement system. This is also a good choice for behaviors that occur only once or twice per day, but that can last for long periods of time (e.g., tantrums).

Latency

In other instances, the critical factor is the amount of time that passes prior to the initiation of the response. For example, your teenage son is expected to feed the dog every night. You may find that you make the first request at 5:00 and then find yourself repeating this request more and more frequently as 6:00 approaches. (You might also find that you are a little less patient each time you make the request.) In this case you want to decrease the time lapse that occurs before your son initiates feeding the dog.

Partial Interval Time Sample

This measurement system allows the observer to simply note whether the behavior occurred within a specified interval of time. Here a block of time is divided into equal segments. For example, a 10-minute period of time could be divided into ten 1-minute intervals, or an hour could be divided into twelve 5-minute intervals. A record is then made of any occurrence of the behavior, be it once or 10 times, within that interval.

Percentage of Opportunities

This is a useful system of measurement when the number of opportunities a person has to engage in a behavior varies from day to day. Here you would keep a tally of both the opportunities presented and the number of times the behavior was exhibited. You would then divide this second number by the first to obtain a percentage. For example, you might be measuring the percentage of opportunities during which a socially withdrawn child established eye contact and greeted others as she walked through the school corridor. You would tally the number of opportunities and the number of times she responded. From this information, you would then calculate the percentage.

What are two important reasons for collecting baseline measures on any behavior you wish to change?

1. _____

_____

2. _____

_____

Go back to the beginning of Step 2 to check your answers.

Now think of at least one behavior that you would like to reduce that could be measured with each of the following data collection options.

Permanent Product: _____

_____

_____

Frequency: _____

_____

_____

Rate: _____

_____

_____

Duration: _____

_____

_____

(continues)

Latency: _____

_____

_____

Partial Interval Time Sample: _____

_____

_____

Percentage of Opportunities: _____

_____

Remember that you want to obtain a representative sample of the behavior. You do not need to measure the behavior all day; rather you want to identify a time or activity during which the behavior is likely to occur. You are encouraged to graph the data collected to allow for a visual display of the current level of the behavior. Along the vertical axis you display the level of the behavior, and along the horizontal axis you display the passage of time, be it days, sessions, or some other measure of time. In the following example, a teacher graphed the number of protests shouted by a child in a preschool program.

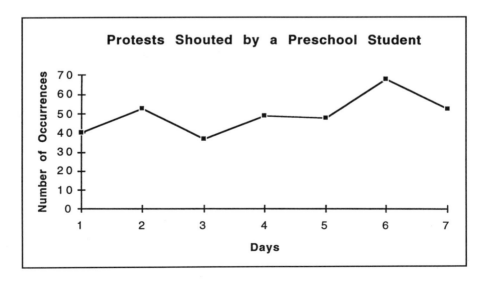

Now graph the behavior or behaviors you assessed in Step 2 that you have chosen to change using a response cost procedure. This will give you a visual representation of the baseline level of the behavior and will help you to see if the behavior changes once you begin implementing response cost.

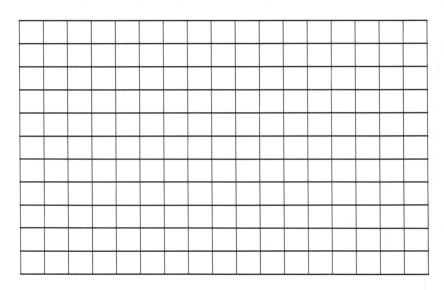

▶ **Step 3: Identify a range of reinforcers.**

When using response cost, it is important to first identify the reinforcer. Remember that reinforcement is particular to the individual and therefore you cannot assume that what impacts one person's behavior will have the same effect on another. To identify potential reinforcers, it is helpful to first observe the individual. What is it that he or she appears to be most interested in? What objects are most often chosen for play? How does the individual spend his or her time? What topics are most often raised in conversation? It is also helpful to ask the person what it is he or she most likes. (For a more in-depth review of reinforcement, refer to *Managing Behavior: Basic Principles*, Hall, 1975.) Whatever is identified, remember that something is a reinforcer only if it strengthens the behavior it follows.

What are three potential reinforcers that could be incorporated into a response cost strategy?

1. _____

   _____

2. _____

   _____

3. _____

   _____

Did you observe the individual in order to find potential reinforcers?
Yes ☐   No ☐

Did you ask the person to identify what it is he or she likes most?
Yes ☐   No ☐

▶ **Step 4: Specify the response cost.**

You next want to identify the level or amount of reinforcement that will be removed contingent upon the targeted response. You want to be sure to find a good balance, choosing an amount that will effectively reduce the likelihood of the person's repeating the targeted behavior, yet that is not so severe as to eliminate all motivation to continue to perform appropriate behaviors.

Consider gradually reducing the behavior over time. If the unwanted behavior occurs at a rate of 10 times per hour, you might want to start by allowing only 5 occurrences or less within this same period of time.

Sam was a student in a special education program. When he first arrived, his teachers were immediately impressed with his high rate of inappropriate vocal behavior. Although Sam was bilingual, he spent much of his time making loud noises. Not only did these noises interfere with his learning, but they also drew odd stares from others, increasing Sam's isolation and limiting the further development of his social skills. The teachers chose a response cost strategy to try to reduce these noises. A "star card" was made up, on which were drawn 62 stars (this was half the average rate observed during baseline measures collected during 30-minute blocks of time). At the beginning of the session, Sam was shown the card while the teacher explained that every time he made a noise, he would lose a star. At the end of 30 minutes, if he had one star left, he would have access to 5 minutes of taped music. Most days this was in place, Sam made 61 or fewer noises and thereby enjoyed the music. Over time the teachers were able to decrease the number of stars available across longer periods of time, until eventually Sam made only a few noises over several hours (adapted from Rotholz & Luce, 1983).

In this example, the teachers first identified a potentially reinforcing activity that they could add to Sam's schedule. Music was chosen as it appeared that Sam enjoyed the auditory stimulation that his noises produced. They next chose a level of cost that they believed would be effective, yet acceptable. Fortunately, this proved to be true, as supported by Sam's behavior. (Again, this highlights the importance of collecting measures on any behavior you wish to change.) Had the teachers chosen a response cost that was too extreme, the procedure would not have been effective and they would have adjusted the program accordingly.

At other times, you may want to consider a hierarchy of cost, with more serious rule violations resulting in greater loss than minor infractions.

Lee was a student in Mr. Nolan's alternative class at the high school. According to school records, Lee's presenting problems included swearing, threatening others, fighting, and skipping class. Mr. Nolan had developed a system in which students could earn points for appropriate behavior and, conversely, lose them for unwanted behavior. After collecting baseline measures on the behaviors he had specified, Mr. Nolan decided to implement a response cost contingency immediately. As he was most concerned with those responses that posed a risk of injury to others, he decided that Lee would be fined accordingly: fighting, 200 points; threatening others, 150 points; skipping class, 100 points; and swearing, 75 points.

Describe a behavior that could be reduced gradually using a response cost strategy.

_____

_____

_____

(continues)

Identify four behaviors that could all be targeted for reduction but that would result in differing levels of response cost (develop a hierarchy of response cost).

1. _____

_____

_____

2. _____

_____

_____

3. _____

_____

_____

4. _____

_____

_____

Check your selections with a colleague or with a professional acting as your instructor.

▶ Step 5: Implement the response cost contingency.

Now that you have specified the behavior, collected baseline measures, identified the reinforcer, and determined the level of loss, it is time to implement the strategy. You want to be sure to communicate the rules of response cost to the person with whom you are working. You also want to be sure to carry out the contingency in a calm and quiet manner. Simply remove the privilege, point, or token. It is not necessary to provide further comment as you have already explained the rules. This helps avoid arguments or discussion that may inadvertently provide reinforcement in the form of attention to the unwanted behavior.

Max was a 10-year-old boy who had been diagnosed with attention-deficit/hyperactivity disorder and conduct disorder. He displayed a number of problem behaviors, including aggression, property destruction, and swearing. After taking baseline measures, the teachers at Max's school had devised a point system designed to reduce these problems while teaching Max some self-control. The day was divided into naturally occurring blocks of time (i.e., 9–11 arrival until lunch, 11–12 lunch and recess, 1–3 recess until departure). Assigned to each block of time were 5 points. As long as Max did not display any of his targeted problem behaviors, he kept all of his points. If he did engage in aggression, destruction, or swearing, he lost 1 point and was sent to a time-out chair. As long as he sat in the chair, he kept the remaining points. If he refused to sit in the chair or left the chair without permission, he lost all of the points remaining in that time block. Max was motivated to earn as many points as he could as his parents gave him a dime for each point he brought home from school. This system was in place instead of an allowance.

An analysis of Max's problem behaviors indicated that at least part of his motivation was to gain attention from adults. Prior to implementing the response cost contingency, the teachers explained the rules to Max. Although he protested initially when points were removed, his teachers ignored his comments and quietly went about their work. Once he was again behaving appropriately, they provided positive feedback in the form of attention. After a few days, Max rarely protested when he lost a point.

What are two rules to remember when using response cost?

1. _____

_____

_____

2. _____

_____

_____

If you stated that you should communicate the rules of response cost to everyone involved and that you should remove the reinforcer in a calm and quiet manner, you're on the right track.

▶ **Step 6: Evaluate the effectiveness of the procedure.**

To understand whether response cost is having the desired reductive effect on the behavior you have targeted for change, it is important to continue measuring the behavior. In this way you can compare the rate of the behavior with and without response cost. Continue to graph your data so that you have a clear picture of the behavior. Be sure to draw a vertical line between your baseline data and the data you collect after you begin using response cost.

Have you observed a suppression in the targeted behavior? If so, the response cost procedure is having the desired effect.

▶ **Step 7: Maintain the change.**

As is true with any positive change in behavior, the goal is to maintain this change using the most natural strategies possible. Ideally, reductions in unwanted behavior will be maintained as more positive behavior is reinforced. As Sam made fewer strange noises, people were able to engage him in social conversation, thereby providing him with a significant amount of attention that proved motivating to him. As the students in the high school program displayed significantly fewer interfering behaviors, they began attending to their studies, developing greater skills and receiving praise from staff and family members for a job well done. You are advised to ensure that this enhanced access to reinforcement does indeed occur. As you observe fewer instances of the problem behavior, do not forget to continue to offer intermittent or occasional positive reinforcement for appropriate, alternative behavior.

▶ **Step 8: Ensure generalization.**

On occasion you may observe a reduction in the unwanted behavior in one setting or during one activity only. To facilitate the generalization of the effect across all pertinent environments, it may be necessary to systematically apply the response cost strategy across additional settings. Be sure to apply response cost only where the behavior is unacceptable. (For more information on generalization, see *How To Plan for Generalization*, Baer, 1981, or *An Operant Pursuit of Generalization*, Stokes and Osnes, 1989.)

Luke was a 4-year-old diagnosed with pervasive developmental disorder. He had been attending an integrated preschool program for approximately 1 year, making significant gains in all areas of development. However, his teacher began to notice that whenever any adult would offer praise or comment on his activity, he would shout in protest. As this proved to be disruptive to the classroom and a behavior that would not be acceptable in most school settings, it was agreed that a plan should be developed to reduce this behavior. As the computer was one of Luke's favorite activities, it was agreed that the intervention would begin during computer time. The frequency of his shouts was recorded to obtain a baseline measure of this response. Next he was provided with 10 stickers on a laminated strip of paper. This number was 5 less than the average number of shouts he made during baseline. Luke was told that he had to have at least one sticker in order to stay at the computer. Then, whenever he shouted, the teacher would simply take one sticker from his board. Very quickly, the rate of shouting decreased. The number of stickers was reduced and this same strategy was extended to other activities and environments, including morning circle and his home (adapted from McIlvin & Thibadeau, 1997).

Review: Steps in Using Response Cost

To review the steps involved in using response cost, identify the step and then provide an example.

Step 1: _____

_____

_____

Step 2: _____

_____

_____

Step 3: _____

_____

_____

Step 4: _____

_____

_____

(continues)

Step 5: _____

_____

_____

Step 6: _____

_____

_____

Step 7: _____

_____

_____

Step 8: _____

_____

_____

Look back to the preceding pages to check whether you have listed the steps correctly.

Benefits of Using Response Cost

1. One of the real benefits of response cost is the relative ease with which it can be employed. Once an appropriate level of loss is identified, it can be applied discreetly, quietly, and without significant disruption to the ongoing activity. This allows you to provide immediate feedback regarding unacceptable behavior, yet allows the individual to remain engaged in the activity and therefore to continue to access reinforcement for appropriate behavior.

2. Research has highlighted the benefits of incorporating response cost into a systematic reinforcement strategy. This procedure has actually enhanced the program's overall effectiveness, helping individuals to discriminate acceptable from unacceptable behavior. With the addition of response cost, a more rapid and significant suppression of problem behavior may be observed, thereby offering greater opportunity for the strengthening of appropriate behavior.

3. Although it involves an aversive consequence to unwanted behavior, response cost is relatively mild and therefore generally acceptable to a range of individuals. Unlike time-out, response cost does not involve the removal of the individual from an activity and, therefore, as noted previously, allows continued access to reinforcement. In comparison to contingent effort procedures, response cost does not involve the presentation of an aversive event. For these reasons alone, parents and educators are more likely to tolerate and accept this treatment contingency.

Review the benefits of using response cost.

1. _____

_____

_____

_____

_____

2. _____

_____

_____

_____

3. _____

_____

_____

_____

_____

Considerations When Using Response Cost

1. As response cost involves the removal of a specified quantity of reinforcement, one runs the risk of creating a situation in which there is an absence of reinforcement. If the individual continues to display unwanted behavior, you may find that eventually all reinforcement is depleted, leaving the individual with nothing to motivate him or her to perform or behave appropriately. Therefore, you should always try to maintain a reinforcement "reserve," or an amount of reinforcement to which the individual still has access. In order to maintain this reserve and maintain motivation, you should always apply reinforcement for appropriate behavior.

The group home staff had been taught to demonstrate some flexibility in their delivery of reinforcement. In particular, they were encouraged to seize any available opportunity to reinforce improvement in their students' behavior. When Cole arrived home from school, he was met by the group home parent, Jack, who wanted to discuss the fight that had occurred at school. Cole acknowledged that he had been involved in a fight and handed over his point card. Jack reminded him that fighting resulted in a loss of 100 points, but then he paused. Jack was very impressed with Cole as he took responsibility for his behavior. He did not protest or swear, as he would have done months earlier. Observing this progress, Jack wanted to reinforce this behavior. After about a minute's delay, Jack told Cole that he had just earned 50 points back because he had appropriately admitted his involvement and accepted the consequences of his actions (adapted from Phillips et al., 1971).

2. The reader is also cautioned to avoid gradually increasing the cost that one forfeits following the unwanted response. Research has demonstrated that individuals may acclimate to the loss of reinforcement if there is a gradual increase in the response cost. You may find that there is little to no change in the problem behavior as the individual has learned to tolerate the loss.

3. Response cost can be most effective when it is used with a program of systematic reinforcement applied to appropriate behavior. In this way the individual is earning privileges, points, or tokens for wanted behavior, while concurrently losing these reinforcers following unwanted behavior. Response cost may also be used as part of a more complex treatment package involving both positive and other negative consequences.

Summary

In this manual, you have been provided with guidelines to help you effectively use response cost to reduce problem behaviors. Behaviors that impede one's development, interfere with the rights of others, or pose a risk to an individual's health and safety are all behaviors that require intervention. The reader is encouraged to use response cost responsibly and only after positive approaches to behavior change have not produced the desired effect or require too long a period of time. Remember to follow these steps when using a response cost strategy:

1. Provide an observable and measurable definition of the behavior.

2. Collect objective measures of the current level of the behavior.

3. Create a graph that depicts the data you have collected.

4. Identify reinforcers that can be removed following the unwanted behavior.

5. Determine the specific amount of reinforcement to be removed.

6. Explain the rules of response cost.

7. Implement the response cost strategy calmly and with limited attention.

8. Be sure to reinforce appropriate behavior.

9. Evaluate the effectiveness of the response cost.

10. Maintain the behavior change.

11. Be sure to extend the results to all appropriate settings and activities.

References and Further Reading

Alexander, R. N., Corbett, T. F., & Smigel, J. (1976). The effects of individual and group consequences on school attendance and curfew violations with predelinquent adolescents. *Journal of Applied Behavior Analysis, 9*, 221–226.

Ayllon, T., & McKittrick, S. M. (1982). *How to set up a token economy*. Austin, TX: PRO-ED.

Baer, D. M. (1981). *How to plan for generalization*. Austin, TX: PRO-ED.

Barnard, J. D., Christopherson, E. R., & Wolf, M. M. (1977). Teaching children appropriate shopping behavior through parent training in the supermarket setting. *Journal of Applied Behavior Analysis, 10*, 49–59.

Barrish, H. H., Saunders, M., & Wolf, M. M. (1969). Good Behavior Game: Effects of individual contingencies for group consequences on disruptive behavior in a classroom. *Journal of Applied Behavior Analysis, 2*, 119–124.

Clark, H. B., Greene, B. F., Macrae, J. W., McNees, M. P., Davis, J. L., & Risley, T. R. (1977). A parent advice package for family shopping trips: Development and evaluation. *Journal of Applied Behavior Analysis, 10*, 605–624.

Dougherty, B. S., Fowler, S. A., & Paine, S. C. (1985). The use of peer monitors to reduce negative interaction during recess. *Journal of Applied Behavior Analysis, 18*, 141–153.

Dupaul, G. J., Guevremont, D. C., & Barkley, R. A. (1992). Behavioral treatment of attention-deficit hyperactivity disorder in the classroom—The use of the attention training system. *Behavior Modification, 16*, 204–225.

Epstein, L. H., & Masek, B. J. (1978). Behavioral control of medicine compliance. *Journal of Applied Behavior Analysis, 11*, 1–9.

Fox, D. K., Hopkins, B. L., & Anger, W. K. (1987). The long-term effects of a token economy on safety performance in open-pit mining. *Journal of Applied Behavior Analysis, 20*, 215–224.

Goldstein, R. S., Minkin, B. L., Minkin, N., & Baer, D. M. (1978). Finders, keepers? An analysis and validation of a free-found-ad policy. *Journal of Applied Behavior Analysis, 11*, 465–473.

Hall, R. V. (1975). *Managing behavior: Basic principles* (rev. ed.). Austin, TX: PRO-ED.

Iwata, B. A., & Bailey, J. S. (1974). Reward versus cost token systems: An analysis of the effects on students and teachers. *Journal of Applied Behavior Analysis, 7*, 567–576.

Kaufman, K. F., & O'Leary, K. D. (1972). Reward, cost, and self-evaluation procedures for disruptive adolescents in a psychiatric hospital school. *Journal of Applied Behavior Analysis, 5*, 293–309.

Kazdin, A. E. (1972). Response cost: The removal of conditioned reinforcers for therapeutic change. *Behavior Therapy, 3*, 533–546.

Kazdin, A. E. (1985). The token economy. In R. M. Turner & L. M. Ascher (Eds.), *Evaluating behavior therapy outcome* (pp. 225–253). New York, NY: Springer.

Kazdin, A. E. (1989). *Behavior modification in applied settings*, 4th ed. Homewood, IL: Dorsey Press.

Lippman, M. R., & Motta, R. W. (1993). Effects of positive and negative reinforcement on daily living skills in chronic psychiatric patients in community residences. *Journal of Clinical Psychology, 49*, 654–662.

McIlvin, J. H., & Thibadeau, S. F. (1997). *Reducing the shouted protests of a young child through response cost.* Unpublished manuscript.

McSweeney, A. J. (1978). Effects of response cost on the behavior of a million persons: Charging for directory assistance in Cincinnati. *Journal of Applied Behavior Analysis, 11,* 47–51.

Phillips, E. L. (1968). Achievement Place: Token reinforcement procedures in a home-style rehabilitation setting for "pre-delinquent" boys. *Journal of Applied Behavior Analysis, 1,* 213–223.

Phillips, E. L., Phillips, E. A., Fixsen, D. L., & Wolf, M. M. (1971). Achievement Place: Modification of the behaviors of pre-delinquent boys with a token economy. *Journal of Applied Behavior Analysis, 4,* 45–59.

Piazza, C. C., & Fisher, W. (1991). A faded bedtime with response cost protocol for treatment of multiple sleep problems in children. *Journal of Applied Behavior Analysis, 24,* 129–140.

Rapport, M. D., Murphy, H. A., & Bailey, J. S. (1982). Ritalin vs. response cost in the control of hyperactive children: A within-subject comparison. *Journal of Applied Behavior Analysis, 15,* 205–216.

Reimeres, T. M. (1996). A biobehavioral approach toward managing encopresis. *Behavior Modification, 20,* 469–479.

Reisinger, J. J. (1972). The treatment of "anxiety depression" via positive reinforcement and response cost. *Journal of Applied Behavior Analysis, 2,* 125–130.

Rogers, R. W., Rogers, J. S., Bailey, J. S., Runkle, W., & Moore, B. (1988). Promoting safety belt use among state employees: The effects of prompting and a stimulus-control intervention. *Journal of Applied Behavior Analysis, 21,* 263–269.

Rotholz, D., & Luce, S. C. (1983). The development of alternative strategies for the reduction of self-stimulatory behavior in autistic youth. *Education and Treatment of Children, 6,* 363–377.

Siegel, G. M., Lenske, J., & Broen, P. (1969). Suppression of normal speech disfluencies through response cost. *Journal of Applied Behavior Analysis, 2,* 265–276.

Sulzer-Azaroff, B., & Mayer, G. R. (1991). *Behavior analysis for lasting change.* Fort Worth, TX: Holt, Rinehart and Winston, Inc.

Stokes, T. F., & Osnes, P. G. (1989). An operant pursuit of generalization. *Behavior Therapy, 20,* 337–355.

Switzer, E. B., Deal, T. E., & Bailey, J. S. (1977). The reduction of stealing in second graders using a group contingency. *Journal of Applied Behavior Analysis, 10,* 267–272.

Walker, H. M., Hops, H., & Fiegenbaum, E. (1976). Deviant classroom behavior as a function of combinations of social and token reinforcement and cost contingency. *Behavior Therapy, 7,* 76–88.

Winkler, R. C. (1970). Management of chronic psychiatric patients by a token reinforcement system. *Journal of Applied Behavior Analysis, 3,* 47–55.